This book belongs to

_____

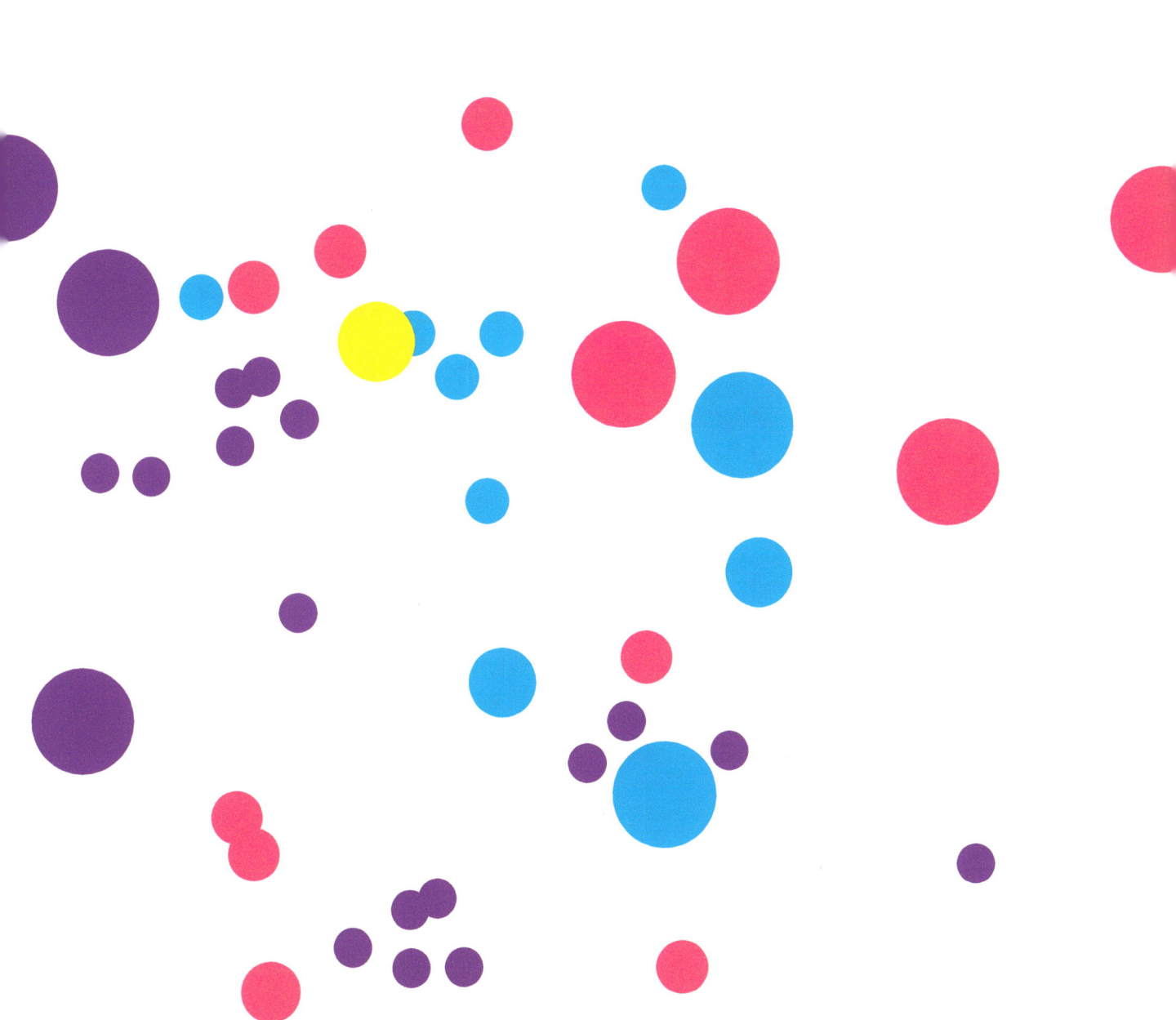

Dedicated to
J & R

SLUSHY

STUCKY

MAYOR JUST RIGHT

CRUSTY

GOBBLEBUM

CURLY

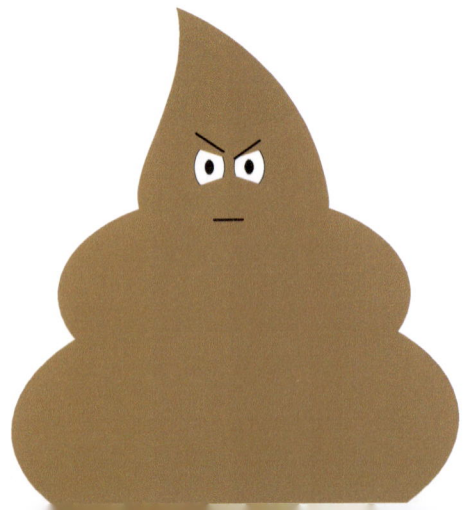

The sun is shining in Potty Hill Town, all is well, and Slushy is taking his sunglasses for a walk.

However, Slushy's feel good factor is about to end.

CRUSTY CALLING

Gobblebum is a **big** dog who eats anything and everything!

"YUM
YUM
I AM
GOBBLEBUM"

Even though Slushy is scared of slobbery Gobblebum, he wants to help Crusty.

So he nervously says *"Sure Crusty, I'll do it!"*

Crusty gives Slushy
a list of instructions
on how to look after
Gobblebum...

JUST KEEP HIM HAPPY! • •

WRITE
YOUR OWN
INSTRUCTIONS
HERE

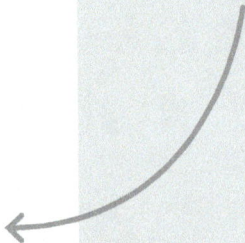

☐

· · · · · · · · · · · · · · · · · ·

☐

· · · · · · · · · · · · · · · · · ·

☐

· · · · · · · · · · · · · · · · · ·

☐

· · · · · · · · · · · · · · · · · ·

☐

· · · · · · · · · · · · · · · · · ·

☐

· · · · · · · · · · · · · · · · · ·

**"YUM
YUM
I AM
GOBBLEBUM"**

As soon as Crusty leaves,

Gobblebum eats the list!!

So, Slushy creates his own list.

- ☑ WALK DOG
- ☐ PEE & POO
- ☐ FEED DOG
- ☐ DOG SLEEPS
- ☐ SLUSHY GOOD FRIEND

They race out of the house for a walk.

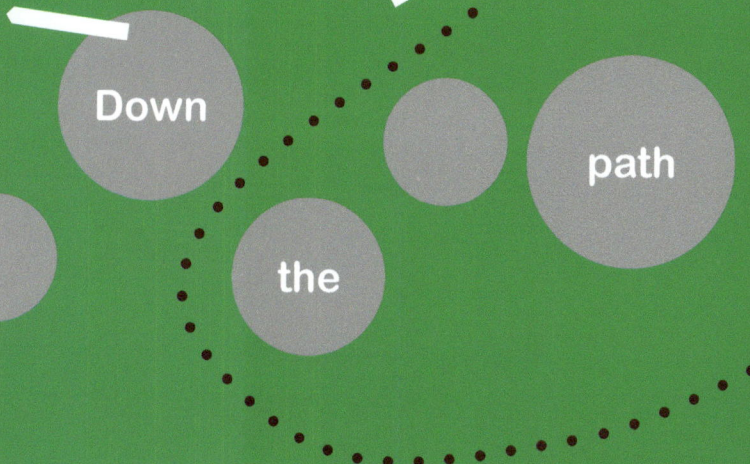

Down the path

Straight into the nearest flower patch.

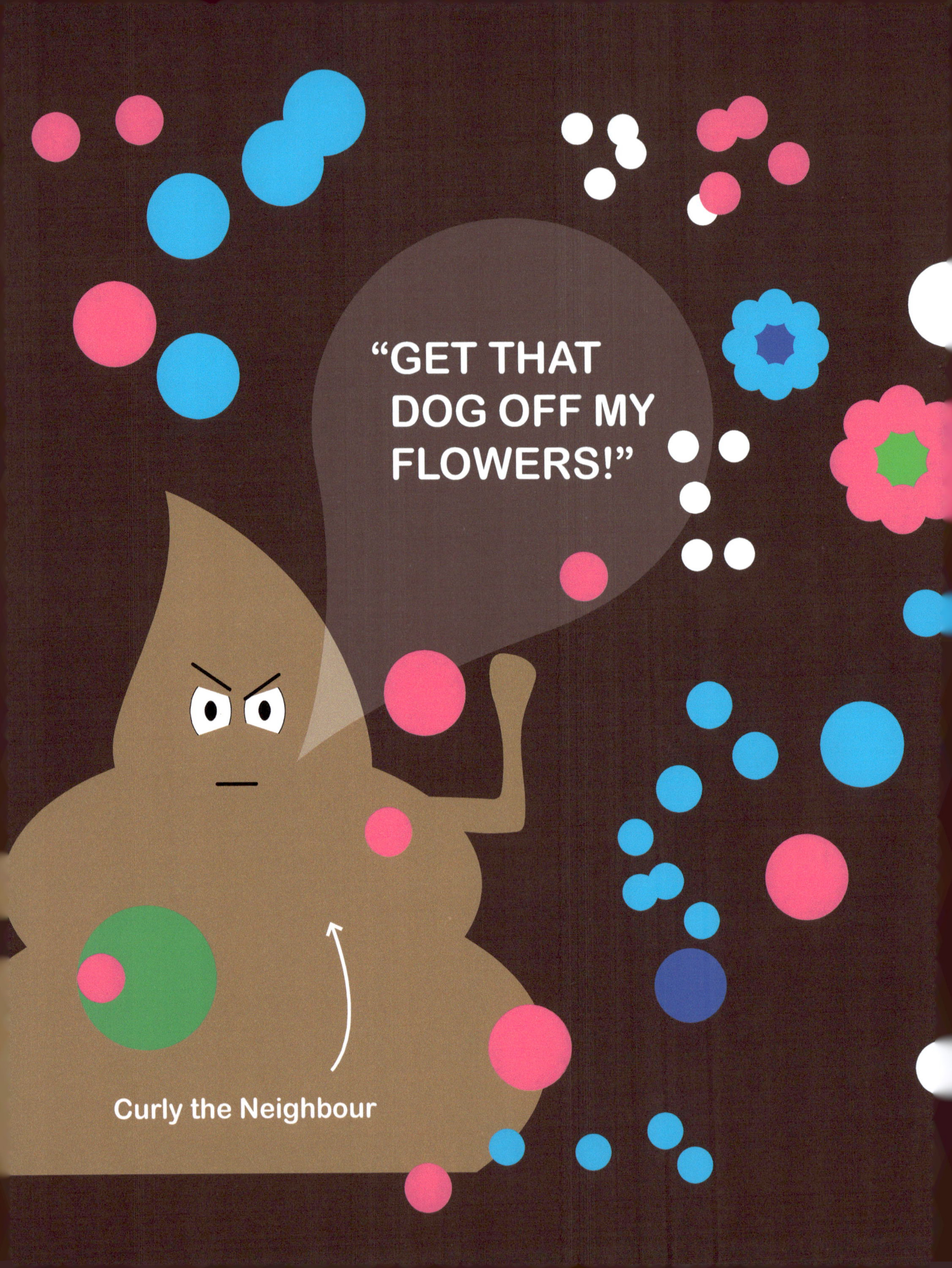
"GET THAT DOG OFF MY FLOWERS!"
Curly the Neighbour

Curly's shouting makes Gobblebum's bum rumble and he deposits a steaming gift on the flower bed.

"I smell flowery"

Next stop is the market...

It does not take long for the naughty dog
to gobble up all the fruit and vegetables.

"YUM
YUM
I AM
GOBBLEBUM"

He also discovers the bins and munches down a...

football

rubber duck

and a ~~left-over~~ **vegan sandwich!**

This all makes Gobblebum feel a little bit queasy!

"TUM TUM GOBBLEBUM"

His bum rumbles again and Curly receives another gift on his lawn, not so firm this time!

It is time for Slushy to call his friends for help.

However, Stucky is unavailable as he is blocking up Sewer Valley.

So, it is down to Mayor Just
Right to advise Slushy

DISCIPLINE - KINDNESS - ROUTINE

Looking after a dog is a big responsibility.

Slushy reads a book on:

Everything there is to know about...

DOGGY DISCIPLINE

Many days later...

Arghhhh!!

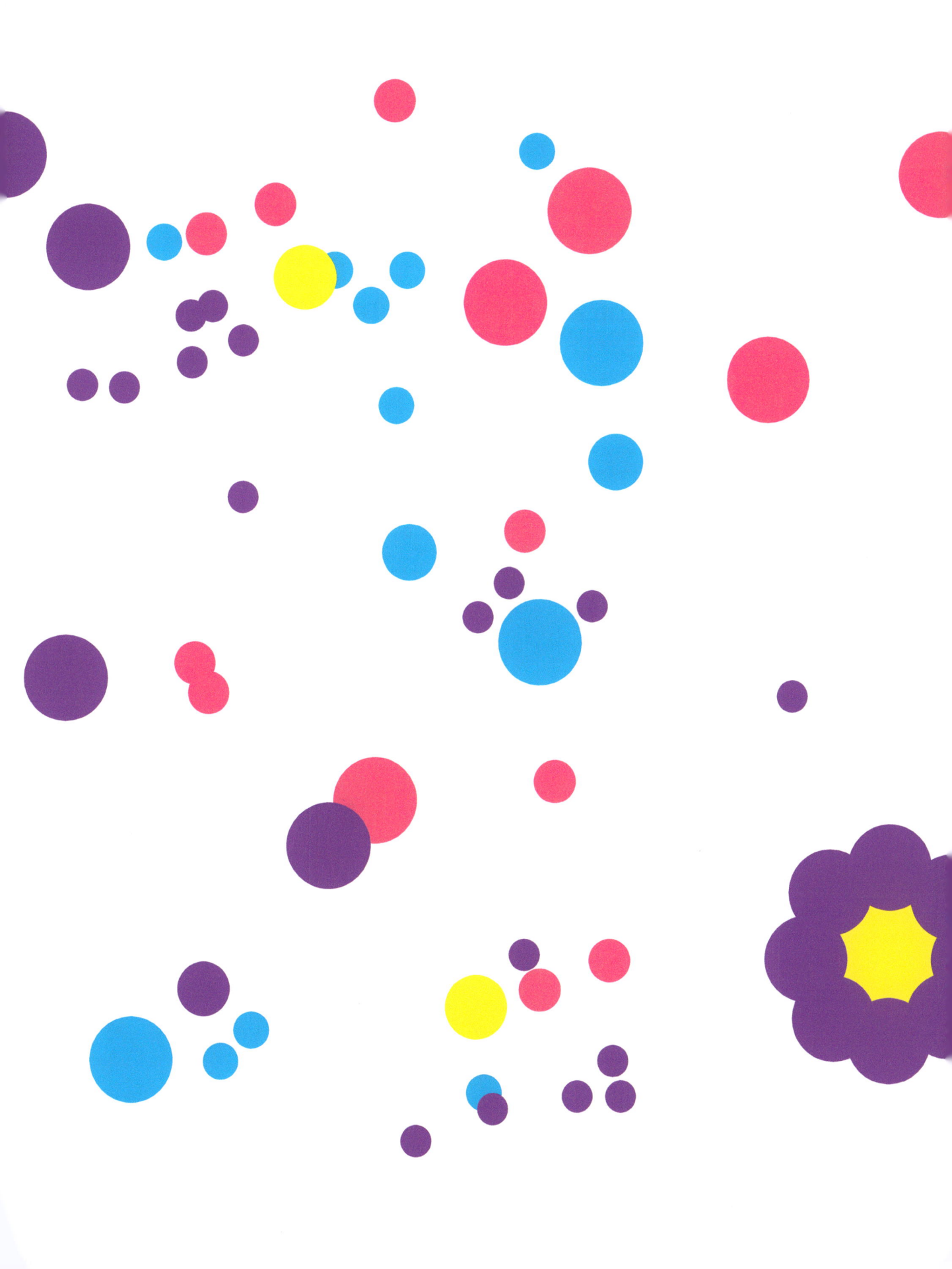

www.ingramcontent.com/pod-product-compliance
Lightning Source LLC
Chambersburg PA
CBHW042127040426
42450CB00002B/101